IOANNIS VASILEIOU

THE EUROPE OF TODAY

BELGIUM, DENMARK, FINLAND, IRELAND, THE NETHERLANDS, NORWAY, POLAND AND SWEDEN

ARE THEY STILL AS DEVELOPED AS THEY SEEM?

ATHENS 2021

ACKNOWLEDGEMENTS
To my beloved father

TABLE OF CONTENTS

Special Thanks

(In Alphabetical Order)
To The 17 Following Brilliant Contributors
For Their Excellent Cooperation

Heidi Albertsen [Supermodel,
Actress, Health Advocate, Author, Goodwill
Ambassador, Environmentalist
(www.heidialbertsen.com,
Instagram: @HeidiAlbertsen,
Facebook: /Official.Heidi.Albertsen;
Twitter: @HeidiAlbertsen)]

Dr. Maria Christodoulou, Brussels

Oksana Fedorova [Supermodel,
Miss Russia 2001, Miss Universe 2002,
Writer, Designer, TV Presenter, Actress and
Singer (Website: https://fedorovaoksana.com/)]

Vicky Gerothodorou [Lyricist, Writer, Radio Producer, Entrepreneur, Owner/CEO of Maze Music Productions and Former Top Model (Instagram: https://www.instagram. com/vickygerothodorou/)]

Kalomira [Singer-3rd place at the Eurovision Song Contest-Winner of Fame Story Greece (Website: https://www.kalomira.com/ – Instagram: https://www.instagram. com/itskalomira/)]

Nina Lotsari [Singer-Actress (Website: http:// www.lotsarinina.com/ – Instagram: https:// www.instagram.com/ninalotsariofficial/)]

Maro Lytra [Singer-Fame Story Greece Runner-Up (YouTube: https://www.youtube.com/c/ MaroLytraOfficial/featured – Facebook: https:// el-gr.facebook.com/marolytraofficial – Instagram: https://www.instagram.com/marolytras1/)]

Angelina Mataliotaki [Supermodel, Actress, TV Presenter (Instagram: https://www.instagram.com/angelinamataliotaki/?hl=el – Facebook: https//www.facebook.com/angelina.mataliotaki – Agency: https://www.vnmodels.eu)]

Kei Moreno [Photographer, Former Supermodel, 2002 World Super Model, Author and Creator/ Art Director of Nuts for Fashion Magazine (Website: https://www.keimoreno.com)]

Ioanna Papadimitriou [International Model-Miss Young Greece 1994 (Website: http://www.ioannap.com/ – Instagram: https://www.instagram.com/ioannapapadimitriu/ – Facebook: https://www.facebook.com/IoannaPapadimitriu/)]

Evelina Papantoniou [Jewelry Designer-Former Supermodel, Miss Universe Greece (Star Hellas) 2001, Miss Universe 1st Runner-Up 2001 (Website: https://anileve.com/ – Instagram: https://www.instagram.com/anileve_designs/)]

Nikita Preka [Supermodel, Miss World Albania 2018 (Facebook: https://www. facebook.com/pages/category/Public-Figure/ Nikita-Preka-250726585600139/)]

Ksenia Sarina [Supermodel, Top Model Russia-Fashion Awards (Model Award 2018/2019 Russia), Best Fashion Model-Breakthrough of the Year (Best Face 2019) (Missks.pr@gmail. com – Instagram: @KseniaSarina – Twitter: @ KseniaSarina – Facebook: Ksenia Sarina – Youtube: Ksenia Sarina (https://www.youtube.com/user/ bentliable/about?view_as=subscriber and https:// www.youtube.com/watch?v=86lFCG5yb_U&t=2s) – Vk SarinaKsenia (Russia)]

Anastasia Schipanova [Artist, Supermodel, Miss Intercontinental Belarus 2017, Miss Earth Belarus 2018 (Website: www.schipanova.com – Instagram: an_schipanova – Facebook: Anastasia Schipanova)]

Shaya [Performer, Singer, Songwriter, Winner of Pop Stars Greece, Owner of Shaya Creations (Instagram: https://www.instagram.com/shayahansen/)]

Mariah Tibbetts [Supermodel, Miss Cayman Islands Universe 2020 (Instagram: https://www.instagram.com/mariah.tibbetts/ – Website: https://www.misscaymanislandsuniverse.com)]

Marina Tsintikidou [Landscape Architect working for Outside Landscape Architecture (Website: https://www.outside.gr), Former Supermodel, Former TV Presenter, Miss Universe Greece (Star Hellas) 1992, Miss Europe 1992 (Instagram: https://www.instagram.com/marina.tsintikidou/)]

INTRODUCTION-
GENERAL DISCUSSION
ON EUROPE

Europe has always been the subject of meticulous examination by literally countless researchers, authors, scholars and students from all over the globe mainly due to its staggering history, its democratic principles and a certain degree of diversity among its states.

What is more, the disastrous economic crisis which has not yet ended, accompanied by the calamitous phenomenon of climate change and the nightmarish Covid (with its devastating types and sub-groupings) have also provided researchers with additional impetus as regards Europe's methodical scrutiny (Vasileiou, 2013a, 2013b, 2014a, 2014b, 2015, 2017a, 2017b, 2017c, 2017d, 2017e, 2018a, 2018b, 2018c, 2018d, 2019a, 2019b, 2019c, 2019d, 2019e, 2019f, 2019g, 2019h, 2019j,

2019k, 2020a, 2020e, 2020g, 2020j, 2020k, 2021a, 2021b, 2021c and 2021d).

We surely have to point out that this particular kind of research is something we have also managed to carry out in the context of many of our previous books. Of course Covid and climate change affect the entire globe and it is totally impossible for their future impact to be precisely estimated. Nonetheless, in many cases the exact impact on Europe has repeatedly been the subject of numerous and occasionally controversial debates (Vasileiou, 2013a, 2013b, 2014a, 2014b, 2015, 2017a, 2017b, 2017c, 2017d, 2017e, 2018a, 2018b, 2018c, 2018d, 2019a, 2019b, 2019c, 2019d, 2019e, 2019f, 2019g, 2019h, 2019j, 2019k, 2020a, 2020e, 2020g, 2020j, 2020k, 2021a, 2021b, 2021c and 2021d).

In order for everything to be elucidated in the best possible manner from the very beginning, we have to point out that this initial chapter has not been created in order to serve as just an introduction to the book.

On the contrary, its foremost objective is to sufficiently become the starting point of a hopefully interesting general discussion in terms of the continent as a whole. And that is why this chapter is so lengthy.

We would be extremely grateful if this highly multidimensional chapter could actually serve as a functional compass for further and perhaps better future research. And we do not mean solely in the context of politics and economics.

The admittedly high diversity (in many senses) that exists among the European countries provides us with extra stimulus in order to further delve into some truly significant details that over the years have incontestably contributed to the successful shaping of the continent's truly unique identity (Vasileiou, 2013a, 2013b, 2014a, 2014b, 2015, 2017a, 2017b, 2017c, 2017d, 2017e, 2018a, 2018b, 2018c, 2018d, 2019a, 2019b, 2019c, 2019d, 2019e, 2019f, 2019g, 2019h, 2019j, 2019k, 2020a, 2020e, 2020g, 2020j, 2020k, 2021a, 2021b, 2021c and 2021d).

In terms of the following chapters, we attempt to conscientiously analyze the profiles of eight European countries. As the book title reveals, we are talking about four Northern ones (Denmark, Finland, Norway and Sweden), two of the three Benelux ones (Belgium and the Netherlands), Ireland and Poland.

With the exception of Norway, all the others are EU member states. In addition to that, we have to highlight the fact that Belgium and the Netherlands are EEC founding members, while Ireland and Denmark joined in 1973. Finland and Sweden became EU members in 1995 and, nine years later, Poland managed to achieve the same.

What is more, we certainly have to add that Poland is the sole former communist state examined in the context of this book. Based on our hitherto conducted research, we strongly believe that Poland has incontrovertibly served as a useful example of economic progress ever since its entrance in the Union.

Should we take into account its pre-entrance situation and the numerous adverse tribulations this country experienced from WW2 onwards, we can argue that its current growth and development seem like a miracle.

Another issue that deserves attention is that, apart from its evident economic and social development, Europe can also be regarded as the home place of high fashion, music and arts in general. Some voices might contest this view, but in our opinion, the entire world has been clearly influenced by Europe with respect to the abovementioned sectors.

In addition to that, we strongly believe that the aforesaid sectors can surely be regarded as absolutely pivotal in terms of not only economic progress but also culture, civilization and life quality.

Consequently, in the context this book, these issues will be meticulously analyzed based on some incontestably valid opinions. As the reader will notice in the following paragraphs, a number of famous personalities express some highly interesting points of view with respect to fashion, music and arts in general.

It is also worth mentioning that some of their opinions refer to countries outside Europe, but as the reader will realize, these have been added for two reasons.

The first is to provide the reader with deeper knowledge and the second in order for a comparison between Europe and non-European countries to efficaciously become a reality. The opinions expressed in the context of this chapter are not about the eight case studies of this book but about either Europe as a whole or some member states that are not further examined in this book. We repeat that we have included these opinions for further knowledge.

Fedorova (2021) is a famous supermodel, writer, designer, TV presenter, actress, singer and Miss Universe of 2002. According to her, in general, Russian fashion has been influenced more by European designers rather than US ones.

In addition to that, she unambiguously states that European fashion has incontestably been influenced by Russian designers. Moreover, Fedorova highlights the fact that, nowadays, it is difficult for a young model to become a "big" name in Russia, but not so difficult for a Russian model to become a "big" name in Europe.

Finally, Fedorova underlines that, nowadays, it is also difficult for a Russian model to become successful in the USA.

Gerothodorou (2021) is an outstandingly successful Greek lyricist, writer, radio producer, entrepreneur and former top model.

According to her, the Greek music of nowadays has been influenced more by US music rather than by European one. What is more, she points out that, in general, Greek fashion has been influenced more by European designers rather than US ones.

Additionally, Gerothodorou clearly notes that European fashion has not been influenced by Greek designers. Apart from that, she underlines that it is irrefutably difficult for a new singer to become a "big" name in Greece nowadays.

Finally, Gerothodorou unambiguously states that it is exceedingly difficult for a Greek singer to become a "big" name in Europe nowadays.

Kalomira (2021) is a famous Greek-US singer. According to her, nowadays, it is extremely difficult for a new singer to become a "big" name in the US. What is more, she meticulously adds that, nowadays, it is also tremendously difficult for a Greek singer to become successful in either Europe or the US.

However, despite the difficulties, Kalomira unambiguously states that with hard work and dedication anything is possible, especially now with so many outlets like, inter alia, youtube and instagram. These days the audience is bigger than ever with the world wide web, therefore, the possibilities are endless.

Lotsari (2021) is a tremendously successful singer and actress. According to her, the Greek music of nowadays has been influenced more by European music rather than US one.

Moreover, she points out that, in general, Greek music has failed to influence the US one.

Apart from that, Lotsari carefully underlines that, nowadays, it is indubitably difficult for a new singer to become a "big" name in Greece. Finally, she meticulously highlights the fact that, these days, it is very difficult for a Greek singer to become successful in either Europe or the US.

Lytra (2021) is a famous Greek-Canadian singer. According to her, Greek music has been influenced both by European and American pop, whereas she does not believe that Greek music has actually influenced the American one.

However, she meticulously underlines that there have been songs like "Pump It" from the Black Eyed Peas that she believes has used a sample of "Misirlou" and a song from Rihanna ("Run This Town") that used a guitar solo sample from a Greek player (Greek song).

Apart from that, Lytra clearly notes that, nowadays, it is extremely difficult for a new singer to become a "big" name in the USA, Canada or Europe. Additionally, she mentions that, nowadays, it is also tremendously difficult for a Greek singer to become successful in either Canada or the US.

Mataliotaki (2021) is a supermodel as well as a highly successful actress and TV presenter. Based on her opinion, in general, Greek fashion has been influenced more by European designers rather than US ones. However, she carefully underlines that it has also maintained its own identity as well as influences from the Greek civilization and from numerous periods over time.

Mataliotaki argues that Greek fashion can incontestably be characterized by modern perceptions but which manage to successfully bring certain elements from the past. She also highlights the fact that, as far as Greek fashion is concerned, in a way, the new always includes the old.

Moreover, Mataliotaki points out that Greece is characterized by brilliant fashion designers and she finds it possible that they have indeed inspired European fashion. In addition to that, she notes that this precise inspiration is highly probable to have somehow influenced European fashion.

Mataliotaki adds that, for sure, the Greek civilization and in particular the Ancient Greek one has always been (and will continue being) an inspiration source. This is irrefutably fair should we take its classic beauty into careful consideration.

Apart from that, Mataliotaki states that, nowadays, it is difficult it for a young model to become a "big" name in Greece. Nonetheless, if you have luck, beauty, kindness and courage, it is indeed possible. Mataliotaki says that it is much harder to maintain your fame and many times it is even more difficult to convince yourself that it is incontestably worth doing it.

Furthermore, Mataliotaki highlights the fact that, at present, it is also difficult for a Greek model to become a "big" name in Europe. Nevertheless, again, with luck, charisma, enough willingness and sacrifices, this is indeed possible.

Finally, Mataliotaki notes that COVID-19 came faster (in our lives) than the chase for the American dream. This resulted in the alteration with respect to her business plans and forced her to postpone her stay in New York. She guesses that, these days, it will be difficult for a Greek model to become successful in the US but surely not impossible. Just like everything in life.

Moreno (2021) is a famous photographer as well as a former supermodel. According to her, US fashion has been influenced by European as well as Latin American designers. What is more, she clearly states that, depending on the trends, US fashion has also been influenced by Asian designers.

Apart from that, Moreno highlights the fact that, during her modeling career, it was incontestably difficult for a young model to become a "big" name and not just in the US. And she points out that this depended on numerous factors.

Finally, Moreno underlines that, nowadays, it is not so difficult for a non-US photographer to become successful in the US, but carefully notes that this depends on what is the precise definition of successful.

Papantoniou (2020) is an outstandingly successful Greek jewelry designer as well as a former supermodel.

According to her, in general, Greek fashion has not been influenced by German designers.

On the contrary, she strongly believes that ancient and modern Greek fashion have incontrovertibly been a great influence for all the other countries. In addition to that, she meticulously underlines that Greek fashion has undeniably been influenced by French designers.

What is more, Papantoniou unambiguously states that, during the 2000-10 period, it was not so difficult for a non-German model to build a successful career in Germany. And she also argues that the combination of hard work and persistence was the recipe for success.

Also, with respect to the same period, Papantoniou points out that it was not so difficult for a non-French model to build a successful career in France either.

In order to be more precise, she informs us that the majority of models in Paris are foreigners (mostly from East European countries and Brazil). Nonetheless, she expresses the opinion that for Greek models it was rather difficult.

Apart from that, Papantoniou meticulously notes that that, as a jewelry designer, her work has indubitably been influenced by French designs but not by German ones.

Furthermore, she carefully highlights the fact that the French are characterized by an impeccable style in everything. And she clearly emphasizes that she loves the chic, elegant lines of French fine jewelry designers such as "JAR".

Another outstandingly significant element provided to us by Papantoniou is the fact that if she could choose between France and Germany, in terms of working conditions, she would irrefutably choose the latter. And she sufficiently explains her choice by noting that in Germany working conditions are excellent.

Finally, if she could choose between France and Germany, in terms of quality of life, she would actually choose both. As far as Germany is concerned, Papantoniou mentions that it is unquestionably characterized by a great quality of life, but she also highlights the fact that her all-time favorite city in the world is Paris.

Preka (2021) is a supermodel. According to her, in general, Albanian fashion has been influenced more by European designers rather than US ones. Moreover, she underlines that Albanian fashion has not been influenced by Asian designers but has indeed been influenced by Greek ones.

Apart from that, Preka highlights the fact that, nowadays, it is not so difficult either for a young model to become a "big" name in Albania or for a non-US model to become successful in the US.

Sarina (2021) is a supermodel. She is also a) Top Model Russia (the best Fashion Model of Russia 2018-The Best Face of the fashion model of Russia 2019), b) Miss Earth Ambassador 2018, c) Miss Earth Crimea 2018, d) Silver Medalist East Europe-National Costume Couturier-V.M. Zaitseva, e) Miss Culture & Tourism World Austria (Best Image

Awards Russia 2019), f) Miss World University Emissary Top-10 Russia, g) winner of Peace Emissary Awards-NETIZEN and h) Miss Word Tourism Queen International Russia.

What is more, Sarina is a philanthropist and likes protecting nature and helping animals and children. She is working in Fashion Weeks worldwide (Paris-Paris Fashion week, Italy-Milan Fashion Week, London-London Fashion Week, Asia and NYC-New York Fashion Week), Catwalks and Top Beauty Contests all over the world.

Sarina has repeatedly appeared in numerous tremendously significant fashion magazines such as SOLIZ Paris, Runway Paris, Vogue, Elle, De Mode and Irk. In addition to that, she is the face of many brands and cooperates with world brands and fashion houses around the world.

Sarina regularly decorates Fashion Week World Seasons Worldwide, reputable publications and fashion houses. She has starred for Vogue, Elle, Glamour, In style, Moda, Dolores, Mini and has been the face of the international brand Yffa. She has also worked with numerous other outstandingly notable brands.

Apart from that, Sarina studies French and English at

Moscow State University. At the moment, she is studying and developing her future projects.

According to her, Russian fashion was influenced as a part of American designers by about 50% and the same percentage by European ones. Russian design is versatile in our time and Sarina chooses more eco-friendly brands. She is developing eco-friendly T-shirts with young designers that will soon appear in her style and further in an eco-friendly campaign for her new project. In addition to that, she unambiguously states that European fashion has been influenced by Russian designers.

Also, Sarina underlines that, nowadays, it is very difficult for a young model to become a "big" name in Russia. However, it is possible and worked for her. Sarina is a fighter by nature and probably loves the truth (what you really are, what you can work on and whether you can show results).

She loves the work of a model and the fashion world and she is grateful to all her loved ones who believe in her and support her. For Sarina, beauty is not limited to appearance (clothes and makeup) but she believes it is inside us.

She loves Paris due to the fact that it was the first city where she went to work as a model. At that time, she did not know French and spoke a little English. Now, she is fluent in both languages.

Moreover, she worked at fashion weeks in Paris and other European countries such as Italy. She has been shooting for brands with famous photographers and she is working on new contracts and brands of fashion week. There is a lot of modeling work ahead and it is coming soon.

Sarina's foremost target was to work in Paris, appear at top international beauty contests and work at fashion weeks. Numerous offers began to come in, but once she received offers to work in Paris with which she was in love since the age of three (when a neighbor named Masha gave her a book about the French capital), her dream became a reality.

As soon as she went to Paris, contracts from all over the world, modeling agencies, agents, brands, scouts and top of the world modeling agencies, paid the salary to a promising blonde with brown eyes, golden hair and natural beauty.

Sarina will share with everybody in her modeling dnvnik and will also share new projects. She will continue to cooperate in modeling life full speed ahead to new heights.

Sarina's most important statement is the following: "Be sure with respect to what you wanted and be sure about yourself. Fashion is not just beauty, it is about good attitude. You have to believe in yourself and be strong". She also loves natural beauty.

Based on Sarina's opinion, it is difficult for a Russian model to become successful in the USA these days. Nonetheless, she argues that it is indeed possible to achieve a good result. The main prerequisite for this objective is to work hard in order to get results and go forward.

The recipe of success according to Sarina can be summarized as follows: "Don't stop but go ahead in full speed, never give up, be yourself, be natural, succeed, and move to the future". Sarina considers herself to be a model by vocation and a fighter by nature.

Sarina continues to study and develop in the field of modeling. She works with new European and US modeling agencies, appears in fashion weeks, works with fashion brands and houses, and moves only forward.

She is also paying great attention to highly important environmental problems. In the near future, humanity may face a global catastrophe and its consequences can be irreversible for everyone who lives on planet Earth.

Sarina has been previously engaged in and supported eco-projects of international level. In addition to that, she participated in international actions, within the framework of the international Miss Earth contest.

Schipanova (2021) is a famous artist as well as a supermodel. According to her, in general, Russian painting has been influenced more by European painters rather than US ones. In addition to that, she carefully notes that Russian painting has not been influenced by Greek painters.

Moreover, Schipanova points out that, nowadays, it is not so difficult for a young painter to become a "big" name in Russia. On the contrary, she underlines that, nowadays, it is indeed difficult for a Russian painter to become successful in either Western Europe or the US.

Shaya (2021) is a famous performer, singer and songwriter. According to her, the Greek music of nowadays been influenced more by US music rather than by European one.

In addition to that, she strongly believes that, in general, Greek music has influenced both US and European music.

Moreover, Shaya clearly states that, nowadays, it is very difficult for a new singer to become a "big" name in Greece and also it is very difficult for a Greek singer to become successful in either Europe or the US.

Tibbetts (2021) is a supermodel. She clearly notes that, in general, the fashion of the Cayman Islands has been influenced more by US designers rather than European ones. In addition to that, she underlines that it has not been influenced by South American designers.

What is more, Tibbetts argues that US fashion has indeed been influenced by Latin American designers. Finally, she highlights the fact that, nowadays, it is very difficult for a non-European model to become a "big" name in Europe and for a non-US model to become successful in the US.

Tsintikidou (2021) is a tremendously successful Greek landscape architect as well as a former supermodel and TV presenter. According to her, in general, Greek fashion has been influenced more by European designers rather than US ones.

In addition to that, she unambiguously states that European fashion has incontestably been influenced by Greek designers. What is more, Tsintikidou carefully highlights the fact that, during her modeling career, it was not so difficult for a young model to become a "big" name in Greece.

Also, she meticulously underlines that nowadays it is not easier for a young model to become a "big" name in Greece if compared to the period when she was a model.

Finally, Tsintikidou clearly notes that, during her modeling career, it was extremely difficult for a Greek model to become successful in either Europe or the US.

According to an anonymous interviewee (2021), France's current economic situation can incontestably be regarded as satisfactory. What is more, as far as the UK's current economic situation is concerned, she points out that it is extremely heartening.

Apart from that, the interviewee clearly notes that Greek fashion has indubitably been influenced by both French and British designers.

Moreover, she underlines that if she compares France and the UK in terms of working environment, no difference can actually be observed. On the contrary, if she compares the two abovementioned countries with respect to quality of life, France is indeed better.

We strongly believe that the abovementioned points of view have provided the reader with highly interesting information with respect to fashion, music and arts in general.

What is more, this truly multidimensional combination of opinions can offer the reader the chance for an interesting critical comparison which will possibly lead to several fruitful conclusions. In addition to that, this comparison might provide the reader with stimulus for future research.

As a general conclusion, we would surely argue that, over the years, Europe has been characterized by a higher degree of political, social and economic stability, if compared for example to Africa, Asia or South America (Vasileiou, 2013a, 2013b, 2014a, 2014b, 2015, 2017a, 2017b, 2017c, 2017d, 2017e, 2018a, 2018b, 2018c, 2018d, 2019a, 2019b, 2019c, 2019d, 2019e, 2019f, 2019g, 2019h, 2019j, 2019k, 2020a, 2020e, 2020g, 2020j, 2020k, 2021a, 2021b, 2021c and 2021d).

The exception of course is the recent worldwide economic and financial crisis and the nightmarish scourges of climate change and Covid, but these have affected the entire globe as well (Vasileiou, 2013a, 2013b, 2014a, 2014b, 2015, 2017a, 2017b, 2017c, 2017d, 2017e, 2018a, 2018b, 2018c, 2018d,

2019a, 2019b, 2019c, 2019d, 2019e, 2019f, 2019g, 2019h, 2019j, 2019k, 2020a, 2020e, 2020g, 2020j, 2020k, 2021a, 2021b, 2021c and 2021d).

The precise method of analysis of which this book has been based is similar to the one that has already been used in the context of some of our previous ones. This actually means that that the overall efficaciousness of this method has repeatedly been tested. And we dare to argue that, thus far, the outcomes have indeed been heartening (Vasileiou, 2013a, 2013b, 2014a, 2014b, 2015, 2017a, 2017b, 2017c, 2017d, 2017e, 2018a, 2018b, 2018c, 2018d, 2019a, 2019b, 2019c, 2019d, 2019e, 2019f, 2019g, 2019h, 2019j, 2019k, 2020a, 2020e, 2020g, 2020j, 2020k, 2021a, 2021b, 2021c and 2021d).

Apart from the introduction, this book comprises four chapters. The first three concern the eight case studies, whereas the last one summarizes the most significant concluding remarks.

More specifically, Chapter 1 is titled *"Northern Europe: The Cases of Denmark, Finland, Norway and Sweden"*. Chapter 2 is named *"Belgium and the Netherlands: Stability and Progress Even in Problematic Times"*, while the title of Chapter 3 is *"Ireland and Poland: Growth in a Difficult Era"*.

In the context of the three aforesaid chapters, the structure and the targets in general are more or less similar in order to provide the reader with the opportunity to make comparisons more easily.

We have attempted to simplify the chapters as much as possible and eliminate all the scientific details that might eventually become somewhat perplexing.

In order to be more specific, with respect to the chapters in question, we attempt to provide the reader with some necessary general information and then to methodically focus on a number of specific features in terms of the increasingly interesting political systems of our case studies.

At the same time, we proceed to a critical presentation of a wealth data which refer to numerous pivotal issues and characteristics ranging from total area and population to ethnic groups, languages, religions, population growth rates and urban population.

What is more, we have also succeeded in discovering equally salient information as regards GDP real growth rates, industrial production growth rates, unemployment rates, population below poverty line and inflation rates.

Additionally, we attempt to scrupulously examine miscellaneous equally matters that are linked with either the economic or the sociopolitical sphere in terms of a continuous effort to efficaciously establish a sufficient framework of analysis.

Just like in our previous books, our foremost target is not the superficial presentation of quantitative data, but a deep analysis which attempts to highlight an enormous spectrum of incontestably crucial elements (Vasileiou, 2013a, 2013b, 2014a, 2014b, 2015, 2017a, 2017b, 2017c, 2017d, 2017e, 2018a, 2018b, 2018c, 2018d, 2019a, 2019b, 2019c, 2019d, 2019e, 2019f, 2019g, 2019h, 2019j, 2019k, 2020a, 2020e, 2020g, 2020j, 2020k, 2021a, 2021b, 2021c and 2021d).

One of the principal aims of this book is to familiarize the reader with some sectors or fields where, in our opinion, the future planning of our eight case studies must be primarily focused.

Finally, in Chapter 4, the main *"Concluding Remarks"* are being painstakingly highlighted, in order for a satisfactory synopsis with respect to the most substantial arguments on which this book has been based to become a reality.

In order for this goal to be reached, the already achieved targets are being conscientiously presented, the current difficulties and tribulations are being meticulously noted and the foremost future prospects are being systematically scrutinized.

CHAPTER 1

NORTHERN EUROPE: THE CASES OF DENMARK, FINLAND, NORWAY AND SWEDEN

With respect to this chapter, we will critically focus on Denmark, Finland, Norway and Sweden in order to reach a number of fruitful conclusions as regards their current situation and some of their foremost future perspectives.

It is widely accepted that Northern Europe has always been one of the most significant areas in terms of democracy, education, security, economic and financial growth, political stability and social harmony.

What is more, we must not forget that the majority of the Northern European states (if not all) rank very high in terms of equality, living standards, healthcare, life quality and happiness.

Denmark is our first step of analysis and we have to mention that it is a developed country with increasingly notable living standards. Its sole border country is Germany (Encyclopedia "Domi", Vol. 7; Encyclopedia "The Counselor of the Young", Vol. 4; Purnell History of the 20th Century, 1968, Vol. 1, 2, 4, 5 and 6; World History 1, 1990).

Denmark can be regarded as a constitutional monarchy. It is characterized by a representative parliamentary system with a head of government (the prime minister) as well as a head of state (the monarch) who officially retains executive power, despite the fact that duties are strictly representative and ceremonial. Moreover, we must take into account that the kingdom also consists of two autonomous constituent countries in the Atlantic, neither of which are EU members (Greenland and the Faroe Islands) (Europa/Denmark, 2020).

Its total area is 43,094 sq km and we have to point out that it includes the island of Bornholm in the Baltic Sea as well as the rest of metropolitan Denmark (the Jutland Peninsula, and the major islands of Sjaelland and Fyn), but excludes the Faroe Islands and Greenland [Country Comparison to the

World (CCW): 134]. Its population is 5,869,410 (July 2020 est.) (CCW: 115) (CIA Factbook/Denmark, 2020).

Its capital city is Copenhagen, while other notable cities and towns are Aarhus, Odense, Aalborg, Esbjerg, Randers, Kolding, Horsens, Vejle, Roskilde, Herning, Silkeborg, Fredericia, Viborg, Holstebro, Taastrup, Slagelse, Svendborg, Frederikshavn, Ringsted, Haderslev and Skive (Encyclopedia "Domi", Vol. 7; Encyclopedia "The Counselor of the Young", Vol. 4; Purnell History of the 20th Century, 1968, Vol. 1, 2, 4, 5 and 6; World History 1, 1990).

The ethnic groups in Denmark are the following: a) Danish (includes Greenlandic (who are predominantly Inuit) and Faroese) 86.3%, b) Turkish 1.1% and c) other 12.6% (largest groups are Polish, Syrian, German, Iraqi, and Romanian) (2018 est.) (data represent population by ancestry). Moreover, the languages in Denmark are Danish, Faroese, Greenlandic (an Inuit dialect) and German (small minority). We also have to underline that English is the predominant second language (CIA Factbook/Denmark, 2020; Encyclopedia "Domi", Vol. 7; Encyclopedia "The Counselor of the Young", Vol. 4; World History 1, 1990).

Religions in Denmark are a) Evangelical Lutheran (official) 74.7%, b) Muslim 5.5% and c) other/none/unspecified (denominations of less than 1% each in descending order of size include Roman Catholic, Jehovah's Witness, Serbian Orthodox Christian, Jewish, Baptist, Buddhist, Mormon, Pentecostal, and nondenominational Christian) 19.8% (2019 est.) (CIA Factbook/Denmark, 2020; Encyclopedia "Domi", Vol. 7; Encyclopedia "The Counselor of the Young", Vol. 4; World History 1, 1990).

Its population growth rate is 0.48% (2020 est.) (CCW: 157), while its urban population 88.1% of the total (2020). Its GDP real growth rate was 2.3% (2017 est.), 2% (2016 est.) and 1.6% (2015 est.) (CCW: 139). Its industrial production growth rate is 2.5% (2017 est.) (CCW: 116). Its unemployment rate was 5.7% (2017 est.) and 6.2% (2016 est.) (CCW: 84), while its population below poverty line is 13.4% (2011 est.) (excludes students). Finally, its inflation rate (consumer prices) was 1.1% (2017 est.) and 0.3% (2016 est.) (CCW: 58) (CIA Factbook/Denmark, 2020).

As we can observe, the percentage of Denmark's urban population is extremely high, while some truly encouraging features incontestably comprise a) its steady increase of its GDP real growth rate between 2015 and 2017, b) its notable reduction with respect to its unemployment rate between 2016 and 2017 and c) its very low (although increasing) inflation rate (consumer prices) from 2016 to 2017.

Denmark has been an EU member since 1/1/1973, while we also have to highlight that it has actually negotiated an opt-out from the euro, hence, it is not obliged to introduce it. Moreover, it has been a Schengen area member since 25/3/2001 (Europa/Denmark, 2020).

There are 12 members of the European Parliament from Denmark, while we must also add that as far as the presidency of the Council of the EU is concerned, the dates of Danish presidency were from a) July to December 1973, b) from January to June 1978, c) July to December 1982, d) July to December 1987, e) January to June 1993, f) July to December 2002 and g) January to June 2012 (Europa/Denmark, 2020).

In addition to that, we must not forget that Denmark has nine representatives on the European Economic and Social Committee and the same number on the European Committee of the Regions. In 2018, the total EU spend in

Denmark reached €1.411 bn (equivalent to 0.46% of the Danish economy), while the total contribution to EU budget was €2.541 bn (equivalent to 0.83% of the Danish economy) (Europa/Denmark, 2020).

According to Albertsen (2021), Denmark is experiencing a temporary economic lull caused by the pandemic. However, she remains highly optimistic for its future as it pertains to its people, public health, the economy, and prospects for continued prosperity and happiness.

Albertsen is adamant that Denmark continues to benefit from its entrance into the EU and its increased strategic economic ties within the Union.

She argues that Denmark has had considerable export trade with Germany, which has consistently experienced growth. With its healthy and sustainable economy, Germany has proven a critical economic driver benefitting Denmark, she adds.

Albertsen lives both in England and the USA. Following Brexit, England's departure from the EU brings a new dynamic that she finds far from positive. She underscores that the EU has provided people with flexibility and opportunities concerning a) jobs, b) imports and exports, and c) convenient travel.

Albertsen points out that it is beneficial for Denmark to be a part of the EU as its membership yields numerous advantages: a) increased choice and stable prices for consumers and citizens, b) greater security and more opportunities for businesses and markets, c) improved economic stability and growth, d) more integrated financial markets, e) a more substantial presence for the EU in the global economy, and f) a tangible sign of a European identity.

Albertsen argues that the 2004-2014 period presented some dark times for her native homeland. Specifically, she notes that 2008 was a tremendously negative time for all due to the economic collapse and global financial crisis. She concludes that the 2015-19 period showed vast improvement in Denmark's economic growth compared to 2004-14.

Albertsen noted that BNP Paribas characterizes 2015-20 as among the most significant periods for economic growth within Denmark. However, she states that the year 2020 brought a temporary pause in that growth, as the pandemic damaged multiple industries and hampered economic activity.

As far as the current relationship between Denmark and Russia is concerned, Albertsen observes that it is less than ideal. In contrast, Denmark and the USA's relationship offers more promise from an economic, cultural, and geopolitical standpoint. She bases her opinion on the existence of multiple trade agreements and a greater degree of shared values between the two nations.

The relationship between Denmark and the USA has been well-established since WW2, and Denmark has consistently aligned with the USA as an active member of the United Nations and through contributions in conflict areas and zones.

Moreover, Albertsen supports the fact that Denmark's entrance into the EU has attracted more tourists. Regarding today's Danish agricultural and industrial sectors, she mentions that they are both experiencing considerable growth. And she also notes that Denmark produces excellent butter and cheese from world-class dairy milk, which have long been emblematic of Danish culture.

Also, she states that Denmark is known as one of the world's leading nations. The country prioritizes that everyone is treated equally under the law and that help is available to anyone and everyone in need. Economic growth, development, and democracy are more than evident than in many other nations. It is one of the top countries in which to raise a family due to its excellent, resource-abundant educational system that consistently ranks among the best in Europe. Its higher education system, she notes, is consistently ranked among the best in the world.

Albertsen highlights the role of the prime minister and the Royal family throughout its history. She argues that Denmark is one of the world's oldest countries and offers a rich history stemming from the Viking era -- a great source of pride for modern-day Danes. She notes that the Vikings pioneered shipbuilding technology, enabling travel previously thought impossible, which led to the world's transformation.

She also emphasizes that the Danish flag is one of the oldest in history, appropriate for a nation so proud of its roots, and that Denmark is perhaps the world's happiest country. Albertsen asserts that happiness is closely linked to social equality and community spirit, citing the World Happiness Report, which is based on polling from Gallup. Denmark fares well by these metrics.

Based on Albertsen's opinion, Denmark is characterized by a high level of equality and a strong sense of common responsibility concerning social welfare.

Friis (2002) argues that Denmark and the EU seem like a married couple that back in 1998 managed to celebrate their silver wedding and adds that their relationship at the time this article was being authored could actually be characterized as far from smooth.

More specifically, Friis methodically highlights the fact that the Danish electorate voted no in two tremendously salient EU referenda (in 1992, voters actually rejected the Maastricht Treaty and eight years later said no with respect to the country's participation in terms of the single currency). Such an element is incontestably worth noting for numerous rather obvious reasons.

Helgertz et al. (2014) underline in the most emphatic manner the particular (and increasing) notability with respect to the naturalization of immigrants in Europe.

In order to be more precise, they attempt to systematically compare the naturalization impact as regards the income attainment of immigrants in Denmark and Sweden via the methodical use of longitudinal register data from 1986 till the time their article was authored.

The conclusion is that, as far as Sweden was concerned, rather insignificant obstacles to naturalization could be observed. On the contrary, in the case of Denmark, more pronounced naturalization barriers were evident (Helgertz et al., 2014).

Hansen et al. (2016) methodically estimate the amount of Danish households that were indeed willing to pay for home, auto and house insurance at the time their article was being authored.

The conclusion drawn was that the actual willingness to pay was in reality slightly higher compared to the actuarially fair value under expected utility theory. Nonetheless, it was notably higher under rank-dependent utility theory and up to 600% higher compared to the actuarially fair value (Hansen et al., 2016).

Our examination continues with Finland, which borders Sweden, Norway and Russia. It is also a developed country, despite the fact that till the 1950s, it could be somehow characterized as a rather agrarian one (Encyclopedia "Domi",

Vol. 27; Encyclopedia "The Counselor of the Young", Vol. 9; Purnell History of the 20th Century, 1968, Vol. 1-5; World History 2, 1990).

Some voices might contrast this specific view, but we remain certain about it based on our hitherto conducted research. What is more, it ranks high in the context of tremendously prominent issues such as life quality and education (Encyclopedia "Domi", Vol. 27; Encyclopedia "The Counselor of the Young", Vol. 9; Purnell History of the 20th Century, 1968, Vol. 1-5; World History 2, 1990).

Finland is a parliamentary republic with a head of government (the prime minister) as well as a head of state (the president). What is more, we have to note that the central government is based in Helsinki, while the local governments in the 311 municipalities (towns and cities). In addition to that, it is surely worth mentioning that the country is divided into 19 regions and 70 sub-regions (Europa/Finland, 2020).

Its total area is 338,145 sq km (CCW: 66) and its population 5,571,665 (July 2020 est.) (CCW: 116) (CIA Factbook/Finland, 2020).

Its capital city is Helsinki, while other notable cities are Espoo, Tampere, Vantaa, Oulu, Turku, Jyvaskyla, Lahti, Kuopio, Pori, Lappeenranta, Vaasa, Kotka, Joensuu, Hameenlinna, Porvoo, Mikkeli, Hyvinge, Jarvenpaa, Nurmijarvi, Rauma, Mellunkyla, Lohja, Vuosaari, Kokkola, Kajaani, Rovaniemi, Tuusula and Kirkkonummi (Encyclopedia "Domi", Vol. 27; Encyclopedia "The Counselor of the Young", Vol. 9; Purnell History of the 20th Century, 1968, Vol. 1-5; World History 2, 1990).

The ethnic groups in Finland are Finn, Swede, Russian, Estonian, Romani and Sami. The languages in Finland are a) Finnish (official) 87.6%, b) Swedish (official) 5.2%, c) Russian 1.4% and d) other 5.8% (2018 est.). Furthermore, religions in Finland are a) Lutheran 69.8%, b) Greek Orthodox 1.1%, c) other 1.7% and d) unspecified 27.4% (2018 est.) (CIA Factbook/ Finland, 2020; Encyclopedia "Domi", Vol. 27; Encyclopedia "The Counselor of the Young", Vol. 9; Purnell History of the 20th Century, 1968, Vol. 1-5; World History 2, 1990).

Its population growth rate is 0.3% (2020 est.) (CCW: 171), while its urban population 85.5% of the total (2020). Its GDP real growth rate was 2.8% (2017 est.), 2.5% (2016 est.) and

0.1% (2015 est.) (CCW: 122). Its industrial production growth rate is 6.2% (2017 est.) (CCW: 39). Its unemployment rate was 8.5% (2017 est.) and 8.8% (2016 est.) (CCW: 121). Its inflation rate (consumer prices) was 0.8% (2017 est.) and 0.4% (2016 est.) (CCW: 41) (CIA Factbook/Finland, 2020).

As we can notice, the percentage of Finland's urban population is tremendously high, while some really heartening elements include a) its ceaseless increase as regards its GDP real growth rate between 2015 and 2017, b) its decrease with respect to its unemployment rate from 2016 to 2017 and c) its outstandingly low (although slightly increasing) inflation rate (consumer prices) between 2016 and 2017.

Finland has been an EU member since 1/1/1995, a Euro area member since 1/1/1999 and a Schengen area member since 25/3/2001 (Europa/Finland, 2020).

There are 13 members of the European Parliament from Finland, while we must also add that as far as the presidency of the Council of the EU is concerned, the dates of Finnish presidencies were from a) July to December 1999, b) July to December 2006 and c) July to December 2019 (Europa/Finland, 2020).

Moreover, we must also underline that Finland has nine representatives on the European Economic and Social Committee and the same number on the European Committee of the Regions. In 2018, the total EU spend in Finland reached €1.478 bn (equivalent to 0.63% of the Finnish economy), while the total contribution to EU budget was €2.018 bn (equivalent to 0.87% of the Finnish economy) (Europa/Finland, 2020).

Norway is our third Northern European case study and its border countries are Sweden, Finland and Russia. It is the sole case study of this book that is not an EU member. It is a wealthy country and also ranks high in terms of security, life quality and happiness (Encyclopedia "Domi", Vol. 19; Encyclopedia "The Counselor of the Young", Vol. 7; Purnell History of the 20th Century, 1968, Vol. 1, 4, 5 and 6; World History 2, 1990).

Its total area is 323,802 sq km (CCW: 69) and its population 5,467,439 (July 2020 est.) (CCW: 119) (CIA Factbook/ Norway, 2020).

The ethnic groups in Norway are the following: a) Norwegian 83.2% (includes about 60,000 Sami), b) other

European 8.3% and c) other 8.5% (2017 est.). Moreover, the languages in Norway are Bokmal Norwegian (official), Nynorsk Norwegian (official) and small Sami- and Finnish-speaking minorities. In addition to that, we certainly have to note that Sami has three dialects (Lule, North Sami, and South Sami)[1]. Religions in Norway are a) Church of Norway (Evangelical Lutheran - official) 70.6%, b) Muslim 3.2%, c) Roman Catholic 3%, d) other Christian 3.7%, e) other 2.5% and f) unspecified 17% (2016 est.) (CIA Factbook/Norway, 2020; Encyclopedia "Domi", Vol. 19; Encyclopedia "The Counselor of the Young", Vol. 7; Purnell History of the 20th Century, 1968, Vol. 1, 4, 5 and 6; World History 2, 1990).

Its population growth rate is 0.85% (2020 est.) (CCW: 123), while its urban population 83% of the total (2020). Its GDP real growth rate was 1.9% (2017 est.), 1.1% (2016 est.) and 2% (2015 est.) (CCW: 156). Its industrial production growth rate is 1.5% (2017 est.) (CCW: 143). Its unemployment rate was 4.2% (2017 est.) and 4.7% (2016 est.) (CCW: 56). Finally, tts inflation rate (consumer prices)

1.*We also have to note that Sami is an official language in nine municipalities in Norway's three northernmost counties (Finnmark, Nordland, and Troms).*

was 1.9% (2017 est.) and 3.6% (2016 est.) (CCW: 99) (CIA Factbook/Norway, 2020).

The foremost conclusions that can be drawn from the scrutiny of the abovementioned data can indeed be summarized as follows: a) the percentage of Norway's urban population is tremendously high, b) an almost double increase as regards its GDP real growth rate became a reality between 2016 and 2017, despite the fact that an almost equal reduction took place from 2015 to 2016, c) a significant decrease with respect to its unemployment rate was evident between 2016 and 2017 and d) an almost double reduction as regards inflation rate (consumer prices) took place between 2016 and 2017.

Its capital city is Oslo while other notable cities are Bergen, Trondheim, Fredrikstad, Stavanger, Kristiansand, Skien, Sandnes and Tromso (Encyclopedia "Domi", Vol. 19; Encyclopedia "The Counselor of the Young", Vol. 7; Purnell History of the 20th Century, 1968, Vol. 1, 4, 5 and 6; World History 2, 1990).

Sweden is the final country scrutinized in this chapter. Its border countries are Finland and Norway. It is also a developed country and ranks high in terms of education, security, equality, healthcare and life quality in general (Encyclopedia "Domi", Vol. 25; Encyclopedia "The Counselor of the Young", Vol. 9; Purnell History of the 20th Century, 1968, Vol. 1, 2, 4, 5 and 6; World History 2, 1990).

Sweden can be regarded as a constitutional monarchy and parliamentary democracy with a head of government (the prime minister) and a head of state (the monarch) (Europa/Sweden, 2020).

Moreover, we surely have to note that the government exercises executive power, while legislative power is vested in the single-chamber parliament. We also have to underline that Sweden is a unitary state, divided into 20 counties and 290 municipalities (Europa/Sweden, 2020).

Its total area is 450,295 sq km (CCW: 57) and its population 10,202,491 (July 2020 est.) (CCW: 91) (CIA Factbook/Sweden, 2020).

Its capital city is Stockholm, while other notable cities are Goteborg, Malmo, Uppsala, Sollentuna, Sodermalm, Vasteras, Orebro, Linkoping, Helsingborg, Jonkoping, Norrkoping, Huddinge, Lund, Umea, Haninge, Gavle, Boras, Sodertalje, Kungsholmen, Eskilstuna, Solna, Halmstad,

Vaxlo, Karlstad, Bromma and Molndal (Encyclopedia "Domi", Vol. 25; Encyclopedia "The Counselor of the Young", Vol. 9; Purnell History of the 20th Century, 1968, Vol. 1, 2, 4, 5 and 6; World History 2, 1990).

The ethnic groups in Sweden are the following: a) Swedish 80.9%, b) Syrian 1.8%, c) Finnish 1.4%, d) Iraqi 1.4% and e) other 14.5% (2018 est.). Moreover, it is absolutely necessary to note that data represent the population by country of birth. In addition to that, we have to emphasize that the indigenous Sami people are estimated between 20,000 and 40,000. Apart from that, the languages in Sweden are Swedish (official), while we have to underline that Finnish, Sami, Romani, Yiddish, and Meankieli are official minority languages (CIA Factbook/Sweden, 2020; Encyclopedia "Domi", Vol. 25; Encyclopedia "The Counselor of the Young", Vol. 9; Purnell History of the 20th Century, 1968, Vol. 1, 2, 4, 5 and 6; World History 2, 1990).

Religions in Sweden are a) Church of Sweden (Lutheran) 60.2%, b) other (includes Roman Catholic, Orthodox, Baptist, Muslim, Jewish, and Buddhist) 8.5% and c) none or unspecified 31.3% (2017 est.). At this point we have to mention that estimates actually reflect registered members of faith communities eligible for state funding[2]. In addition to that, it is worth noting that an estimated 57.7% of Sweden's population were members of the Church of Sweden in 2018 (CIA Factbook/Sweden, 2020; Encyclopedia "Domi", Vol. 25; Encyclopedia "The Counselor of the Young", Vol. 9; Purnell History of the 20th Century, 1968, Vol. 1, 2, 4, 5 and 6; World History 2, 1990).

Its population growth rate is 0.79% (2020 est.) (CCW: 130), while its urban population 88% of the total (2020). Its GDP real growth rate was 2.1% (2017 est.), 2.7% (2016 est.) and 4.5% (2015 est.) (CCW: 148). Its industrial production growth rate is 4.1% (2017 est.) (CCW: 74). Its unemployment rate was 6.7% (2017 est.) and 7% (2016 est.) (CCW: 101), while its population below poverty line is 15% (2014 est.). Its inflation rate (consumer prices) was 1.9% (2017 est.) and 1.1% (2016 est.) (CCW: 100) (CIA Factbook/Sweden, 2020).

The major conclusions are the following: a) the percentage

---

2. *We have to clarify that not all religions are state-funded and not all people who identify with a particular religion are registered members. This is a highly significant detail that must not go unnoticed.*

of Sweden's urban population is tremendously high, b) an incessant reduction in terms of its GDP real growth rate was taking place between 2015 and 2017, c) a decrease with respect to its unemployment rate was evident between 2016 and 2017 and d) an almost double increase as regards inflation rate (consumer prices) took place between 2016 and 2017.

Sweden has been an EU member since 1/1/1995, while we also have to highlight that it has actually committed to the euro as soon as it fulfils all essential conditions. Furthermore, Sweden has been a Schengen area member since 25/3/2001 (Europa/Sweden, 2020).

There are 20 members of the European Parliament from Sweden, while we must also add that as far as the presidency of the Council of the EU is concerned, the dates of Swedish presidencies were from a) January to June 2001 and b) July to December 2009 (Europa/Sweden, 2020).

In addition to that, we have to point out that Sweden has 12 representatives on the European Economic and Social Committee and the same number on the European Committee of the Regions. Moreover, we must take into account that, in 2018, the total EU spend in Sweden reached €1.814 bn (equivalent to 0.38% of the Swedish economy), while the total contribution to EU budget was €3.303 bn (equivalent to 0.70% of the Swedish economy) (Europa/ Sweden, 2020).

In the following chapter, a conscientious scrutiny of Belgium and the Netherlands takes place. As we will see, these two founding EEC members are good examples of economic progress and social stability but room for improvement always exists.

CHAPTER 2

BELGIUM AND THE NETHERLANDS: STABILITY AND PROGRESS EVEN IN PROBLEMATIC TIMES

In terms of this chapter, we attempt to provide the reader with recent and accurate information on two Benelux countries (Belgium and the Netherlands). As we will see, they can still be characterized by a relatively high degree of growth, stability and social harmony, despite the current difficult times.

To begin with, Belgium is our initial case study and borders France, the Netherlands, Luxembourg and Germany. It is not difficult to understand the outstanding significance of Brussels in terms of politics and economics at a pan-European level (Encyclopedia "Domi", Vol. 5; Encyclopedia "The Counselor of the Young", Vol. 3; Purnell History of the 20th Century, 1968, Vol. 1-6; World History 1, 1990).

What is more, we must not forget to meticulously underline that Belgium can surely be regarded as a developed country and has a very prosperous economy. Apart from that, it ranks high in terms of life quality, safety and healthcare (Encyclopedia "Domi", Vol. 5; Encyclopedia "The Counselor of the Young", Vol. 3; Purnell History of the 20th Century, 1968, Vol. 1-6; World History 1, 1990).

Belgium is a federal constitutional monarchy in which the king is the head of state and the prime minister is the head of government in a multi-party system. What is more, we have to add that decision-making powers are not centralized, but divided between three levels of government: the federal government, three language-based communities (Flemish, French and German-speaking) and three regions (Flanders, Brussels Capital and Wallonia) (Europa/Belgium, 2021).

In addition to that, we certainly have to underline that, legally, they all are equal, but have powers and responsibilities for different fields. Another tremendously notable feature that must not go unnoticed is that Brussels is, together with Luxembourg City and Strasbourg, one of the three official seats of the European institutions (Europa/Belgium, 2021).

Its total area is 30,528 sq km (CCW: 141) and its population 11,720,716 (July 2020 est.) (CCW: 80) (CIA Factbook/Belgium, 2020).

Its capital city is Brussels, while other notable cities are Antwerp, Ghent, Charleroi, Liege, Bruges, Namur, Leuven, Mons, Mechelen, Aalst, La Louviere, Hasselt and Kortrijk (Encyclopedia "Domi", Vol. 5; Encyclopedia "The Counselor of the Young", Vol. 3; Purnell History of the 20th Century, 1968, Vol. 1-6; World History 1, 1990).

The ethnic groups in Belgium are the following: a) Belgian 75.2%, b) Italian 4.1%, c) Moroccan 3.7%, d) French 2.4%, e) Turkish 2%, f) Dutch 2% and g) other 10.6% (2012 est.). The languages in Belgium are a) Dutch (official) 60%, b) French (official) 40% and c) German (official) less than 1%. Moreover, religions in Belgium are a) Roman Catholic 50%, b) Protestant and other Christian 2.5%, c) Muslim 5%, d) Jewish 0.4%, e) Buddhist 0.3%, f) atheist 9.2% and g) none 32.6% (2009 est.) (CIA Factbook/Belgium, 2020; Encyclopedia "Domi", Vol. 5; Encyclopedia "The Counselor of the Young", Vol. 3; Purnell History of the 20th Century, 1968, Vol. 1-6; World History 1, 1990).

Its population growth rate is 0.63% (2020 est.) (CCW: 148), while its urban population 98.1% of the total (2020). Its GDP real growth rate was 1.7% (2017 est.), 1.4% (2016 est.) and 1.4% (2015 est.) (CCW: 162). Its industrial production growth rate is 0.2% (2017 est.) (CCW: 168). Its unemployment rate was 7.1% (2017 est.) and 7.9% (2016 est.) (CCW: 108), while its population below poverty line is 15.1% (2013 est.). Finally, its inflation rate (consumer prices) was 2.2% (2017 est.) and 1.8% (2016 est.) (CCW: 112) (CIA Factbook/Belgium, 2020).

As we can easily notice: a) the percentage of Belgium's urban population is extraordinarily high, b) an increase in terms of its GDP real growth rate took place between 2016 and 2017, c) a significant decrease with respect to its unemployment rate was evident between 2016 and 2017 and d) a slight increase as regards inflation rate (consumer prices) took place between 2016 and 2017.

Belgium has been an EU member since 1/1/1958, a Euro area member since 1/1/1999 and a Schengen area member since 26/3/1995 (Europa/Belgium, 2021).

Apart for that, we have to take into consideration that there are 21 members of the European Parliament from

Belgium, while we must also add that as far as the presidency of the Council of the EU is concerned, the dates of Belgian presidencies were from a) January to June 1958, b) January to June 1961, c) January to June 1964, d) January to June 1967, e) January to June 1970, f) January to June 1973, g) July to December 1977, h) January to June 1982, i) January to June 1987, j) July to December 1993, k) July to December 2001 and l) July to December 2010 (Europa/Belgium, 2021).

Also, Belgium has 12 representatives on the European Economic and Social Committee and 12 on the European Committee of the Regions. In 2018, the total EU spend in Belgium reached €8.514 bn (equivalent to 1.86% of the Belgian economy), while the total contribution to EU budget was €3.840 bn (equivalent to 0.84% of the Belgian economy) (Europa/Belgium, 2021).

According to Christodoulou (2020), in general, Belgium's current economic situation cannot be regarded as particularly heartening. Nonetheless, she indicates that Belgium has incontestably been benefited from the EU and, in our opinion, this is an irrefutably crucial in far too many senses argument.

Moreover, according to Christodoulou the 2004-14 period was the best in terms of economic growth for Belgium, if compared to the 2015-20 one.

Apart from that, in her view, the current relations between Belgium and the USA are likely to be enhanced with Biden administration.

What is more, Christodoulou clearly notes that Belgium's EU membership has attracted more tourists in the country and this is another undeniably significant finding.

As far as today's agricultural and industrial sectors of Belgium are concerned, Christodoulou underlines that they are both currently undergoing significant hardship, but carefully notes that it depends on the product sector.

Finally, Christodoulou points out that, most importantly, following the 6th reform of the State (which started in 2012 and was completed in 2014), Belgium' federal powers in economic and policy terms have been reduced, leaving more space for independent decision-making to the regions (the Brussels Region, Wallonia and Flanders).

Papadimitriou (2020) is a Greek international model. According to her, in general, Greek fashion has not been influenced by either Belgian or Swiss designers.

What is more, she clearly notes that, during the 2000-10 period, it was not so difficult for a non-Belgian model to build a successful career in Belgium and for a non-Swiss one in Switzerland.

Apart from that, Papadimitriou meticulously underlines that, if she could choose between Belgium and Switzerland in terms of working conditions, no particular difference exists between them.

Nonetheless, if she could choose between Belgium and Switzerland, with respect to quality of life, she would indubitably choose the latter.

The Netherlands is the second and final case study of this chapter. It borders Belgium and Germany. Just like Belgium, it is an outstandingly developed country and ranks very high in terms of happiness and life quality (Encyclopedia "Domi", Vol. 20; Encyclopedia "The Counselor of the Young", Vol. 8; Purnell History of the 20th Century, 1968, Vol. 1-6; World History 2, 1990).

The Netherlands is a parliamentary constitutional monarchy with a head of government (the prime minister) as well as a head of state (the monarch). What is more, it is essential to clarify that a council of ministers indeed holds executive power (Europa/Netherlands, 2020).

Furthermore, the country is divided into 12 provinces and 388 municipalities. It is also divided into 22 water districts, governed by an executive board that has authority in matters of water management. In addition to that, the Netherlands includes six overseas countries and territories in the Caribbean which are not part of the Union (Europa/ Netherlands, 2020).

Its total area is 41,543 sq km (CCW: 135) and its population 17,280,397 (July 2020 est.) (CCW: 67) (CIA Factbook/ Netherlands, 2020).

Its capital city is Amsterdam, while other notable cities are Rotterdam, The Hague, Utrecht, Eindhoven, Groningen, Tilburg, Almere, Breda, Nijmegen, Apeldoom, Haarlem, Arnhem, Enschede, Amersfoort, Zaanstad, Haarlmemmermeer, 's-Hertogenbosch, Zwolle and Leiden (Encyclopedia "Domi", Vol. 20; Encyclopedia "The Counselor of the Young", Vol. 8; Purnell History of the 20th Century, 1968, Vol. 1-6; World History 2, 1990).

The ethnic groups in the Netherlands are the following: a) Dutch 76.9%, b) EU 6.4%, c) Turkish 2.4%, d) Moroccan 2.3%, e) Indonesian 2.1%, f) German 2.1%, g) Surinamese 2%, h) Polish 1% and i) other 4.8% (2018 est.). The languages in the Netherlands are Dutch (official). What is more, it is essential to point out that Frisian is an official language in Fryslan province. Also, we have to emphasize that Frisian, Low Saxon, Limburgish, Romani, and Yiddish have protected status under the European Charter for Regional or Minority Languages. In addition to that, we have to underline that Dutch is the official language of the three special municipalities of the Caribbean Netherlands. English is a recognized regional language on Sint Eustatius and Saba, while Papiamento is a recognized regional language on Bonaire (CIA Factbook/Netherlands, 2020; Encyclopedia "Domi", Vol. 20; Encyclopedia "The Counselor of the Young", Vol. 8; Purnell History of the 20th Century, 1968, Vol. 1-6; World History 2, 1990).

Apart from that, religions in the Netherlands are a) Roman Catholic 23.6%, b) Protestant 14.9% (includes Dutch Reformed 6.4%, Protestant Church of The Netherlands 5.6%,

Calvinist 2.9%), c) Muslim 5.1%, d) other 5.6% (includes Hindu, Buddhist, Jewish) and e) none 50.7% (2017 est.) (CIA Factbook/Netherlands, 2020; Encyclopedia "Domi", Vol. 20; Encyclopedia "The Counselor of the Young", Vol. 8; Purnell History of the 20th Century, 1968, Vol. 1-6; World History 2, 1990).

Its population growth rate is 0.37% (2020 est.) (CCW: 166), while its urban population 92.2% of the total (2020). Its GDP real growth rate was 2.9% (2017 est.), 2.2% (2016 est.) and 2% (2015 est.) (CCW: 118). Its industrial production growth rate is 3.3% (2017 est.) (CCW: 96). Its unemployment rate was 4.9% (2017 est.) and 6% (2016 est.) (CCW: 69), while its population below poverty line is 8.8% (2015 est.). Its inflation rate (consumer prices) was 1.3% (2017 est.) and 0.1% (2016 est.) (CCW: 70) (CIA Factbook/Netherlands, 2020).

The foremost conclusions that can be drawn are the following: a) the percentage of the Netherlands' urban population is tremendously high, b) a continuous increase in terms of its GDP real growth rate was taking place between 2015 and 2017, c) a highly significant decrease with respect to its unemployment rate was evident between 2016 and 2017 and d) a notable increase as regards inflation rate (consumer prices) took place between 2016 and 2017.

The Netherlands has been an EU member since 1/1/1958, a Euro area member since 1/1/1999 and a Schengen area member since 26/3/1995 (Europa/Netherlands, 2020).

There are 26 members of the European Parliament from the Netherlands, while we must also add that as far as the presidency of the Council of the EU is concerned, the dates of Dutch presidencies were from a) July to December 1960, b) July to December 1963, c) July to December 1966, d) July to December 1969, e) July to December 1972, f) July to December 1976, g) January to June 1981, h) January to June 1986, i) July to December 1991, j) January to June 1997, k) July to December 2004 and l) January to June 2016 (Europa/Netherlands, 2020).

Furthermore, we have to note that the Netherlands has 12 representatives on the European Economic and Social Committee and 12 on the European Committee of the Regions. In 2018, the total EU spend in Netherlands reached €2.470 bn (equivalent to 0.32% of the Dutch economy), while the total contribution to EU budget was €4.845 bn (equivalent to 0.62% of the Dutch economy) (Europa/Netherlands, 2020).

In the following chapter, two completely EU member states are being painstakingly examined. We are talking about Ireland and Poland.

Nonetheless, despite the enormous array of differences, these two countries have managed to achieve economic progress through numerous difficulties.

The economies of both used to be regarded as less advantaged. However, nowadays, despite the economic crises that are still evident all over the globe, their situation can indeed be characterized as satisfactory.

CHAPTER 3

IRELAND AND POLAND: GROWTH IN A DIFFICULT ERA

In the context of this chapter, we will examine two highly different in far too many senses EU countries. According to numerous voices, Ireland and Poland seem to have almost nothing in common.

Nonetheless, based on our hitherto conducted research, we have actually drawn the conclusion that their common element is that, over the years, they have both experienced numerous difficulties but have eventually succeeded in entering the road of progress.

Poland is a former communist country which suffered a lot from the end of WW2 till the USSR collapse. We will not enter into further details with respect to this period due to the fact that it has been critically analyzed and assessed in the context of literally countless studies.

What we need to highlight, though, is that the years between the USSR collapse and its EU joining were also extremely tough. On the contrary, Ireland was lucky enough not to face any similar tribulations.

Ireland is an outstandingly beautiful island located in the North Atlantic, west of Britain. And the UK is its sole border country (Encyclopedia "Domi", Vol. 12; Encyclopedia "The Counselor of the Young", Vol. 5; Purnell History of the 20th Century, 1968, Vol. 1, 2, 3 and 6; World History 1, 1990).

Ireland is a parliamentary republic that comprises 26 counties. What is more, the head of government (the prime minister) is in fact appointed by the president after nomination by the Lower House (Dail) and exercises executive power (Europa/Ireland, 2020).

Moreover, it is worth highlighting that the head of state (the president) is mainly characterized by ceremonial powers. Finally, we must not forget that the Parliament has two chambers (an Upper and Lower House) (Europa/Ireland, 2020).

Its total area is 70,273 sq km (CCW: 121) and its population 5,176,569 (July 2020 est.) (CCW: 122) (CIA Factbook/Ireland, 2020).

Its capital city is Dublin, while other significant cities and towns are Cork, Limerick, Galway, Waterford, Drogheda, Kilkenny, Wexford, Sligo, Clonmel, Dundalk, Bary, Navan, Ennis, Tralee, Carlow, Naas, Athlone, Letterkenny, Tullamore and Killarney (Encyclopedia "Domi", Vol. 12; Encyclopedia "The Counselor of the Young", Vol. 5; Purnell History of the 20th Century, 1968, Vol. 1, 2, 3 and 6; World History 1, 1990).

The ethnic groups in Ireland are the following: a) Irish 82.2%, b) Irish travelers 0.7%, c) other white 9.5%, d) Asian 2.1%, e) black 1.4%, f) other 1.5% and g) unspecified 2.6% (2016 est.). Moreover, the languages in Ireland are English[3] and Irish (Gaelic or Gaeilge)[4]. Religions in Ireland are a) Roman Catholic 78.3%, b) Church of Ireland 2.7%, c) other Christian 1.6%, d) Orthodox 1.3%, e) Muslim 1.3%, f) other 2.4%, g) none 9.8% and h) unspecified 2.6% (2016 est.) (CIA Factbook/Ireland, 2020; Encyclopedia "Domi", Vol. 12; Encyclopedia "The Counselor of the Young", Vol. 5; World History 1, 1990).

---

3. *Official, the language generally used.*
4. *Official, spoken by approximately 39.8% of the population as of 2016. We also have to add that it is mainly spoken in areas along Ireland's western coast known as gaeltachtai, which are officially recognized regions where Irish is the predominant language.*

Its population growth rate is 1.04% (2020 est.) (CCW: 101), while its urban population 63.7% of the total (2020). Its GDP real growth rate was 7.2% (2017 est.), 4.9% (2016 est.) and 25% (2015 est.) (CCW: 17). Its industrial production growth rate is 7.8% (2017 est.) (CCW: 25). Its unemployment rate was 6.7% (2017 est.) and 8.4% (2016 est.) (CCW: 100), while its population below poverty line is 8.2% (2013 est.). Finally, its inflation rate (consumer prices) was 0.3% (2017 est.) and -0.2% (2016 est.) (CCW: 20) (CIA Factbook/Ireland, 2020).

The major conclusions are the following: a) the percentage of Ireland's urban population cannot be regarded as particularly high, b) a tremendously noteworthy increase in terms of its GDP real growth rate took place between 2016 and 2017, following a colossal reduction between 2015 and 2016, c) a truly significant decrease with respect to its unemployment rate was evident between 2016 and 2017 and d) an increase as regards inflation rate (consumer prices) took place between 2016 and 2017.

Ireland has been an EU member since 1/1/1973, a Euro area member since 1/1/1999 and has indeed negotiated an opt-out from Schengen area (Europa/Ireland, 2020).

There are 11 members of the European Parliament from Ireland, while we must also add that as far as the presidency of the Council of the EU is concerned, the dates of Irish presidency were a) from January to June 1975, b) from July to December 1979, c) from July to December 1984, d) from January to June 1990, e) from July to December 1996, f) from January to June 2004 and g) from January to June 2013 (Europa/Ireland, 2020).

In addition to that, we have to highlight the fact that Ireland has nine representatives on the European Economic and Social Committee and eight on the European Committee of the Regions. In 2018, the total EU spend in Ireland reached €2.064 bn (equivalent to 0.82% of the Irish economy), while the total contribution to EU budget was €02.320 bn (equivalent to 0.92% of the Irish economy) (Europa/Ireland, 2020).

Battel (2003) methodically focuses on the Irish economy and unambiguously supports the fact that since independence back in 1922, this economy has actually evolved from being one of the least advantaged in Europe in the 1980s to eventually double-figure growth rates in the 1990s.

It goes without saying that such an achievement is incontestably staggering and surely calls for increased attention at least in our opinion.

Furthermore, Battel notes that this advancement prompted certain comparisons with the so-called "tiger" economies of the Pacific Rim.

Nonetheless, the author clearly highlights that numerous different perceptions exist with respect to whether this growth could be characterized as sustainable and if it managed to raise inequality, relieved poverty or perhaps it did both.

McCoy (2004-2006) mentions that since the late 1990s, Ireland has consistently ranked among the first five nations in terms of output per capita in purchasing power terms by the OECD. Of course we have to point out that this article was published in the 2004-06 period, therefore, the author's conclusions concern only that specific era.

What is more, the Economist Intelligence Unit managed to declare Ireland to actually have the highest quality-of-life characteristics globally in 2004 (McCoy, 2004-2006). It goes without saying that, without exaggeration, this accomplishment deserves to be praised in the most pronounced manner.

Delaney et al. (2013) manage to draw a tremendously notable conclusion that, at least in our opinion, could be characterized as slightly or totally unknown to many people. More specifically, the three authors note that in the 20th century, the Irish-born population in England has actually been in worse health compared to not only the native population but also the Irish one in Ireland.

This is in reality an act of reversing with respect to the commonly observed healthy migrant effect and incontrovertibly calls for increased attention. This article was published in 2013 and at that time birth cohorts born in Ireland and living in England were indeed healthier compared to the English population (Delaney et al., 2013).

Delaney et al. argue that the substantial Irish migrant health penalty arised mainly with respect to cohorts that were actually born between 1920 and 1960.

Poland is the final case study of this book. Its border countries are Russia (Kalinigrad Oblast), Belarus, Ukraine, the Czech Republic, Slovakia, Lithuania and Germany

(Encyclopedia "Domi", Vol. 23; Encyclopedia "The Counselor of the Young", Vol. 8; Purnell History of the 20th Century, 1968, Vol. 1-6; World History 2, 1990).

Poland is a parliamentary republic with a head of government (the prime minister) as well as a head of state (the president). Moreover, we have to add that the government structure is actually centred on the council of ministers. The country is divided into 16 provinces, mainly based on the country's historic regions (Europa/Poland, 2020).

Its total area is 312,685 sq km (CCW: 71) and its population 38,282,325 (July 2020 est.) (CCW: 37) (CIA Factbook/ Poland, 2020).

Its capital city is Warsaw, while other notable cities are Krakow, Lodz, Wroclaw, Poznan, Gdansk, Szczecin, Bydgoszcz, Bialystok, Katowice, Gdynia, Czestochowa, Radom, Torun, Sosnowiec, Rzeszow, Kielce, Gliwice, Zabrze, Olsztyn, Bielsko-Biala, Bytom, Zielona Gora and Rybnik (Encyclopedia "Domi", Vol. 23; Encyclopedia "The Counselor of the Young", Vol. 8; Purnell History of the 20th Century, 1968, Vol. 1-6; World History 2, 1990).

The ethnic groups in Poland are the following: a) Polish 96.9%, b) Silesian 1.1%, c) German 0.2%, d) Ukrainian 0.1% and e) other and unspecified 1.7% (2011 est.) (represents ethnicity declared first). The languages in Poland are a) Polish (official) 98.2%, b) Silesian 1.4%, c) other 1.1% and d) unspecified 1.3% (2011 est.). At this point it is absolutely essential to underline that data represents the language spoken at home. As the reader will have realized, shares sum to more than 100%. This is simply due to the fact that a number of respondents gave more than one answer on the census[5] (CIA Factbook/Poland, 2020; Encyclopedia "Domi", Vol. 23; Encyclopedia "The Counselor of the Young", Vol. 8; World History 2, 1990).

Furthermore, religions in Poland are a) Catholic 85.9% (includes Roman Catholic 85.6% and Greek Catholic, Armenian Catholic, and Byzantine-Slavic Catholic 0.3%),

---

5. *In addition to that, it is worth mentioning that Poland managed to ratify the European Charter for Regional or Minority Languages in 2009 recognizing Kashub as a regional language, Czech, Hebrew, Yiddish, Belarusian, Lithuanian, German, Armenian, Russian, Slovak, and Ukrainian as national minority languages, and Karaim, Lemko, Romani (Polska Roma and Bergitka Roma), and Tatar as ethnic minority languages. It goes without saying that this issue is highly important for way too many reasons.*

b) Orthodox 1.3% (almost all are Polish Autocephalous Orthodox), c) Protestant 0.4% (mainly Augsburg Evangelical and Pentacostal), d) other 0.4% (includes Jehovah's Witness, Buddhist, Hare Krishna, Gaudiya Vaishnavism, Muslim, Jewish, Mormon) and e) unspecified 12.1% (2017 est.) (CIA Factbook/Poland, 2020; Encyclopedia "Domi", Vol. 23; Encyclopedia "The Counselor of the Young", Vol. 8; World History 2, 1990).

Its population growth rate is -0.19% (2020 est.) (CCW: 210), while its urban population 60% of the total (2020). Its GDP real growth rate was 4.7% (2017 est.), 3% (2016 est.) and 3.8% (2015 est.) (CCW: 60). Its industrial production growth rate is 7.5% (2017 est.) (CCW: 28). Its unemployment rate was 4.9% (2017 est.) and 6.2% (2016 est.) (CCW: 70), while its population below poverty line is 17.6% (2015 est.). Finally, its inflation rate (consumer prices) was 2% (2017 est.) and -0.6% (2016 est.) (CCW: 106) (CIA Factbook/Poland, 2020).

As we can easily notice: a) the percentage of Poland's urban population cannot be regarded as very high, b) a tremendously notable increase in terms of its GDP real growth rate took place between 2016 and 2017, c) a highly significant decrease with respect to its unemployment rate was evident between 2016 and 2017 and d) a notable increase as regards inflation rate (consumer prices) took place between 2016 and 2017.

Poland has been an EU member since 1/5/2004 and it is currently preparing in order to adopt the euro. What is more, it has been a Schengen area member since 21/12/2007 (Europa/Poland, 2020).

There are 51 members of the European Parliament from Poland, while we must also add that as far as the presidency of the Council of the EU is concerned, the dates of Polish presidency were from July to December 2011 (Europa/Poland, 2020).

Apart from that, we have to underline that Poland has 21 representatives on the European Economic and Social Committee and 21 on the European Committee of the Regions. In 2018, the total EU spend in Poland reached €16.350 bn (equivalent to 3.43% of the Polish economy), while the total contribution to EU budget was €3.983 bn (equivalent to 0.84% of the Polish economy) (Europa/Poland, 2020).

Zajicek et al. (1997) meticulously point out that the numerous highly interesting (at least in our opinion) economic reforms that took place in Poland actually managed to result in new and incontestably notable prospects with respect to the economics profession. Of course we must not forget that this article was published back in 1997, hence, the authors refer to that specific period.

Moreover, Zajicek et al. clearly highlight that, following numerous decades of economic isolation, Poland was in reality making great efforts in order to sufficiently integrate not only into the global markets but also into the mainstream in terms of economic thinking.

Rather expectedly, the quickly transforming economic environment led to a certain degree of urgency as regards the sufficient preparation of new key personnel of economists trained in market systems (Zajicek et al., 1997).

As a result, according always to Zajicek et al., that specific situation incontestably called for two equally noteworthy prerequisites. The first was the need for restructuring with respect to the entire business and economic curricula at universities, while the second was the coveted establishment of new (and of course based on the precise needs of the time) social studies programmes at high schools as well as continuing education opportunities for businesspeople (Zajicek et al., 1997).

As we can easily observe, the three authors raise some outstandingly notable issues which unambiguously highlighted the exact situation in Poland in the end of the 20th century.

Based on our thus far conducted research, we have drawn the conclusion that this transformation procedure was irrefutably complicated and was indeed characterized by more than a few slightly thorny issues.

Ziomek (2010) methodically focuses on economics performance and institutional economics in Poland after 1989. Just by mentioning this, we irrefutably realize its enormous notability for more than a few rather obvious reasons.

The author argues that ever since the mid-1990s, Poland actually managed to notice a certain interest with respect to the so-called "heterodox" economics including numerous miscellaneous economic trends apart from "mainstream" economics.

In addition to that, Ziomek meticulously underlines that one of the causes for the development of heterodox economic research was the fact that the theses in terms of the end of the transformation procedure in Poland (that in reality appeared before the end of the 1990s), were in a sense not consistent with the statistical data illustrating the Polish economy state.

In the following and final chapter, the most significant concluding remarks are being methodically summarized with a view to the best possible understanding.

What is more, we have to note that in the context of that chapter a brief comparative analysis between our case studies takes place.

Our dominant aim with respect to this analysis is to offer the reader the much-needed opportunity to become familiar with some of the foremost characteristics of the four case studies on which this book has been based in a truly efficacious manner.

This way, we truly believe that he will be able to gain sufficient knowledge which is highly probable to eventually lead him to the extraction of his personal conclusions and provide him with substantial impetus for further and perhaps better conducted research.

It is obvious that accurate future predictions are totally

impossible. Nonetheless, this does not prevent us from systematically emphasizing a number of the most interesting future prospects with regard to both our case studies.

CHAPTER 4

CONCLUDING REMARKS

In the context of this book, we have actually concentrated on six "traditionally" developed European countries (Belgium, Denmark, Finland, Norway, Sweden and the Netherlands) as well as on Ireland and Poland which eventually managed to enter the road of growth and progress after experiencing a number of difficulties.

What is more, we critically focused on issues such as fashion, music and arts in general, in order to show how Europe has incontestably been highly influential to the rest of the world in these sectors as well.

As we have already mentioned, the aforesaid sectors can be characterized as pivotal with respect to not only economic progress but also culture, civilization and life quality.

We remain certain that the numerous valid opinions by a number of famous personalities which have been presented in the first chapter have managed to justify this argument in the best possible manner.

We would be extremely grateful if this book could somehow become a functional compass with a view to the sufficient exploration for new and perhaps more significant findings in the context of both the economic and the sociopolitical sphere.

And we dare to argue that, according to our information, some of our previous books have indeed managed to inspire a number of people with respect to future research (Vasileiou, 2013a, 2013b, 2014a, 2014b, 2015, 2017a, 2017b, 2017c, 2017d, 2017e, 2018a, 2018b, 2018c, 2018d, 2019a, 2019b, 2019c, 2019d, 2019e, 2019f, 2019g, 2019h, 2019j, 2019k, 2020a, 2020e, 2020g, 2020j, 2020k, 2021a, 2021b, 2021c and 2021d).

In the context of this final chapter, unlike some of our previous books, we will not proceed to a scrupulous comparative analysis with respect to the case studies. On the contrary, a brief comparison will take place in order for us to highlight a few important issues that perhaps elucidate if and to what extent economic development has already taken place (Vasileiou, 2013a, 2013b, 2014a, 2014b, 2015, 2017a, 2017b, 2017c, 2017d, 2017e, 2018a, 2018b, 2018c, 2018d,

2019a, 2019b, 2019c, 2019d, 2019e, 2019f, 2019g, 2019h, 2019j, 2019k, 2020a, 2020e, 2020g, 2020j, 2020k, 2021a, 2021b, 2021c and 2021d).

In the following paragraphs, the comparison in question becomes a reality. The data on which it is based are solely those presented and examined in the previous chapters. No additional data have been used. Our target is not to conclude which country is doing better or worse but to draw some conclusions with respect to individual progress.

In terms of population growth rate (2020 est.), the highest can be observed in Ireland (1.04%), whereas the lowest in Poland (-0.19%). With respect to urban population (% of the total-2020), the highest can be noticed in Belgium (98.1), while the lowest again in Poland (60). We also have to note that the percentage of Ireland is also relatively low (63.7%). On the contrary, the percentages of the rest of the case studies are particularly high, ranging from 83% to 92.2%.

In the context of industrial production growth rate (2017 est.), the highest can be seen in Ireland (7.8%), closely followed by Poland (7.5%). Finland's percentage is also tremendously significant (6.2%) The lowest is evident in

Belgium (0.2%). In the other case studies, the percentages range from 1.5% to 4.1%. In terms of population below poverty line, the percentages of three countries (Poland, Belgium and Sweden) range from 15% to 17.6%, which is incontestably high. However, we have to note that the percentages we have managed to discover are not for the same year.

Furthermore, as regards GDP real growth rate, Ireland is by far in the first position (2017 est.) with a percentage which is almost double compared to that of Poland, which ranks second. At this point, we have to underline that it is irrefutably heartening to observe Ireland and Poland at the top of the list.

Apart from that, as far as unemployment rate is concerned, Finland can be noticed in the first position for 2017, while Norway is characterized by the lowest percentage. The truly encouraging feature, though, is that between 2016 and 2017 a reduction in terms of unemployment became a reality in the context of all our case studies. Finally, with respect to inflation rate (consumer prices), it is relatively low in all our case studies.

Furthermore, we truly believe that if the countries examined in this book continue to efficaciously collaborate not only with each other but also with the EU, their relations are highly probable to eventually become more beneficial.

The positive steps that have gradually become a reality over the years are undoubtedly linked to social cohesion and harmony especially nowadays that the global financial instability combined with numerous nightmarish scourges as the incontestably thorny climate change and the recent devastating Covid makes everything highly problematic (Vasileiou, 2013a, 2013b, 2014a, 2014b, 2015, 2017a, 2017b, 2017c, 2017d, 2017e, 2018a, 2018b, 2018c, 2018d, 2019a, 2019b, 2019c, 2019d, 2019e, 2019f, 2019g, 2019h, 2019j, 2019k, 2020a, 2020e, 2020g, 2020j, 2020k, 2021a, 2021b, 2021c and 2021d).

Room for improvement always exists despite the difficulties. However, in order for us to be capable of sufficiently evaluating any attempts for improvement, we have to be patient and wait for at least five years.

BIBLIOGRAPHY

Albertsen, Heidi (2021), Online interview via
the use of questionnaire (11/2/21).

Anonymous Interviewee (2021), Online interview
via the use of questionnaire (11/1/21).

Battel, Róisín Ní Mháille (2003), "Ireland's
"Celtic Tiger" Economy", *Science, Technology,
& Human Values*, 28 (1), pp. 93-111.

Christodoulou, Maria (2020), Online interview
via the use of questionnaire (11/11/20).

CIA Factbook/Belgium (2020), "The World Factbook:
Europe: Belgium", The World Factbook 2020 (Washington,
DC: Central Intelligence Agency, 2020), available at
https://www.cia.gov/library/publications/the-world-
factbook/geos/print_be.html (accessed on 16/9/20).

CIA Factbook/Denmark (2020), "The World Factbook:
Europe: Denmark", The World Factbook 2020 (Washington,
DC: Central Intelligence Agency, 2020), available at
https://www.cia.gov/library/publications/the-world-
factbook/geos/print_da.html (accessed on 1/9/20).

CIA Factbook/Finland (2020), "The World Factbook:
Europe: Finland", The World Factbook 2020 (Washington,
DC: Central Intelligence Agency, 2020), available at
https://www.cia.gov/library/publications/the-world-
factbook/geos/print_fi.html (accessed on 16/9/20).

BIBLIOGRAPHY

CIA Factbook/Ireland (2020), "The World Factbook: Europe: Ireland", The World Factbook 2020 (Washington, DC: Central Intelligence Agency, 2020), available at https://www.cia.gov/library/publications/the-world-factbook/geos/print_ei.html (accessed on 31/8/20).

CIA Factbook/Netherlands (2020), "The World Factbook: Europe: Netherlands", The World Factbook 2020 (Washington, DC: Central Intelligence Agency, 2020), available at https://www.cia.gov/library/publications/the-world-factbook/geos/print_nl.html (accessed on 16/9/20).

CIA Factbook/Norway (2020), "The World Factbook: Europe: Norway", The World Factbook 2020 (Washington, DC: Central Intelligence Agency, 2020), available at https://www.cia.gov/library/publications/the-world-factbook/geos/print_no.html (accessed on 16/9/20).

CIA Factbook/Poland (2020), "The World Factbook: Europe: Poland", The World Factbook 2020 (Washington, DC: Central Intelligence Agency, 2020), available at https://www.cia.gov/library/publications/the-world-factbook/geos/print_pl.html (accessed on 1/9/20).

CIA Factbook/Sweden (2020), "The World Factbook: Europe: Sweden", The World Factbook 2020 (Washington, DC: Central Intelligence Agency, 2020), available at https://www.cia.gov/library/publications/the-world-factbook/geos/print_sw.html (accessed on 16/9/20).

BIBLIOGRAPHY

Delaney, Liam, Fernihough, Alan and Smith, James P. (2013), "Exporting Poor Health: The Irish in England", *Demography*, 50 (6), pp. 2013-2035.

Encyclopedia "Domi" (in Greek), Vol. 5.

Encyclopedia "Domi" (in Greek), Vol. 7.

Encyclopedia "Domi" (in Greek), Vol. 12.

Encyclopedia "Domi" (in Greek), Vol. 19.

Encyclopedia "Domi" (in Greek), Vol. 20.

Encyclopedia "Domi" (in Greek), Vol. 23.

Encyclopedia "Domi" (in Greek), Vol. 25.

Encyclopedia "Domi" (in Greek), Vol. 27.

Encyclopedia "The Counselor of the Young" (original name: Ο Σύμβουλος των Νέων) (in Greek), Vol. 3.

Encyclopedia "The Counselor of the Young" (original name: Ο Σύμβουλος των Νέων) (in Greek), Vol. 4.

Encyclopedia "The Counselor of the Young" (original name: Ο Σύμβουλος των Νέων) (in Greek), Vol. 5.

Encyclopedia "The Counselor of the Young" (original name: Ο Σύμβουλος των Νέων) (in Greek), Vol. 7.

Encyclopedia "The Counselor of the Young" (original name: Ο Σύμβουλος των Νέων) (in Greek), Vol. 8.

Encyclopedia "The Counselor of the Young" (original name: Ο Σύμβουλος των Νέων) (in Greek), Vol. 9.

Europa/Belgium (2021), "Belgium-Overview", available at https://europa.eu/european-union/about-eu/countries/member-countries/belgium_en (accessed on 14/3/21).

Europa/Denmark (2020), "Denmark-Overview", available at https://europa.eu/european-union/about-eu/countries/member-countries/denmark_en (accessed on 11/9/20).

Europa/Finland (2020), "Finland-Overview", available at https://europa.eu/european-union/about-eu/countries/member-countries/finland_en (accessed on 13/9/20).

Europa/Ireland (2020), "Ireland-Overview", available at https://europa.eu/european-union/about-eu/countries/member-countries/ireland_en (accessed on 11/9/20).

Europa/Netherlands (2020), "Netherlands-Overview", available at https://europa.eu/european-union/about-eu/countries/member-countries/netherlands_en (accessed on 11/9/20).

Europa/Poland (2020), "Poland-Overview", available at https://europa.eu/european-union/about-eu/countries/member-countries/poland_en (accessed on 11/9/20).

Europa/Sweden (2020), "Sweden-Overview", available at https://europa.eu/european-union/about-eu/countries/member-countries/sweden_en (accessed on 13/9/20).

BIBLIOGRAPHY

Fedorova, Oksana (2021), Online interview via
the use of questionnaire (13/5/21).

Friis, Lykke (2002), "The Battle Over Denmark:
Denmark and the European Union",
Scandinavian Studies, 74 (3), pp. 379-396.

Gerothodorou, Vicky (2021), Online interview
via the use of questionnaire (3/3/21).

Hansen, Jan V., Jacobsen, Rasmus H. and Lau, Morten I.
(2016), "Willingness to Pay for Insurance in Denmark",
The Journal of Risk and Insurance, 83 (1), pp. 49-76.

Helgertz, Jonas, Bevelander, Pieter and Tegunimataka,
Anna (2014), "Naturalization and Earnings: A Denmark-
Sweden Comparison", *European Journal of Population/
Revue Européenne de Démoyraphie*, 30 (3), pp. 337-359.

Kalomira (2021), Online interview via the
use of questionnaire (31/3/21).

Lotsari, Nina (2021), Online interview via
the use of questionnaire (24/7/21).

Lytra, Maro (2021), Online interview via
the use of questionnaire (22/3/21).

Mataliotaki, Angelina (2021), Online interview
via the use of questionnaire (18/6/21).

BIBLIOGRAPHY

McCoy, Daniel (2004-2006), "Ireland's Spectacular, If Delayed, Convergence", *Radharc*, 5-7, pp. 181-195.

Moreno, Kei (2021), Online interview via the use of questionnaire (31/5/21).

Nugent, Neill (2012), The Government and Politics of the European Union (translated into Greek) (3rd fully revised edition) (Athens: Savvalas).

Papadimitriou Ioanna (2020), Online interview via the use of questionnaire (2/12/20).

Papantoniou Evelina (2020), Online interview via the use of questionnaire (9/12/20).

Preka, Nikita (2021), Online interview via the use of questionnaire (14/6/21).

Purnell History of the 20th Century (1968) (translated into Greek), Vol. 1.

Purnell History of the 20th Century (1968) (translated into Greek), Vol. 2.

Purnell History of the 20th Century (1968) (translated into Greek), Vol. 3.

Purnell History of the 20th Century (1968) (translated into Greek), Vol. 4.

Purnell History of the 20th Century (1968) (translated into Greek), Vol. 5.

BIBLIOGRAPHY

Purnell History of the 20th Century (1968)
(translated into Greek), Vol. 6.

Sarina, Ksenia (2021), Online interview via
the use of questionnaire (30/7/21).

Schipanova, Anastasia (2021), Online interview
via the use of questionnaire (6/6/21).

Shaya (2021), Online interview via the
use of questionnaire (21/4/21).

Tibbetts, Mariah (2021), Online interview via
the use of questionnaire (28/6/21).

Tsintikidou, Marina (2021), Online interview
via the use of questionnaire (29/3/21).

Vasileiou, Ioannis (2013a), *European Unification-A
Process of Convergence, or Divergence?* (in
Greek) (Athens: Historical Quest).

Vasileiou, Ioannis (2013b), "1980-1999, *European
Union: The Years of Expansion and Enlargement*", *From
Hitler's New Europe to Merkel's Eurozone* (in Greek),
Vol. 1, Historical Archive of Ependytis, pp. 76-95.

Vasileiou, Ioannis (2014a), *European Unification-A Process
of Convergence, or Divergence?* (2nd Edition-Special Edition
for Universities) (in Greek) (Athens: Historical Quest).

Vasileiou, Ioannis (2014b), *The Present and Future*

of the Agricultural Policy of the European Union (in Greek) (Athens: Historical Quest).

Vasileiou, Ioannis (2015), *The Foreign and Security Policy of the European Union-A Critical Approach* (in Greek) (Athens: Historical Quest).

Vasileiou, Ioannis (2017a), *Climate Change: Manageable Problem or Slow Death of the Planet? EU Role and Actions until 2050-The Impact on Greece* (in Greek) (Athens: Historical Quest).

Vasileiou, Ioannis (2017b), *Economic Crisis, Employment and Social Affairs in the European Union-Proposals and Actions to Combat Unemployment* (in Greek) (Athens: Historical Quest).

Vasileiou, Ioannis (2017c), *EU Budget-Issues About the Allocation and Redistribution of Resources in the EU* (in Greek) (Athens: Historical Quest).

Vasileiou, Ioannis (2017d), *European Union and Energy-The Route Towards 2050-Thoughts, Ideas and Conclusions* (in Greek) (Athens: Historical Quest).

Vasileiou, Ioannis (2017e), *The European Union Expansion Into Space* (in Greek) (Athens: Historical Quest).

Vasileiou, Ioannis (2018a), *Climate Change: Manageable Problem or Slow Death of the Planet? European Union Role and Actions until 2050-The Impact on Greece* (The

Greek edition translated into English) (Independently
Published/Amazon KDP-Available through Amazon).

Vasileiou, Ioannis (2018b), *Enterprises in the EU:
Monopolies-Cartels-State Aid-Competition Rules*
(in Greek) (Athens: Historical Quest).

Vasileiou, Ioannis (2018c), *European Union Budget-
Issues About the Allocation and Redistribution of
Resources in the European Union* (The Greek edition
translated into English) (Independently Published/
Amazon KDP-Available through Amazon).

Vasileiou, Ioannis (2018d), *The European Union
Expansion Into Space* (The Greek edition translated
into English) (Independently Published/
Amazon KDP-Available through Amazon).

Vasileiou, Ioannis (2019a), *Canada and Mexico: Trade
Relations with the European Union: Towards an Even
More Functional Cooperation* (Independently Published/
Amazon KDP-Available through Amazon).

Vasileiou, Ioannis (2019b), *China-India-ASEAN-Gulf
Region: Trade Relations with the European Union* (The
Greek edition translated into English) (Independently
Published/Amazon KDP-Available through Amazon).

Vasileiou, Ioannis (2019c), *Economic Crisis, Employment
and Social Affairs in the European Union-Proposals and
Actions to Combat Unemployment* (The Greek edition

translated into English) (Independently Published/ Amazon KDP-Available through Amazon).

Vasileiou, Ioannis (2019d), *Enterprises in the EU-Monopolies-Cartels-State Aid-Competition Rules* (The Greek edition translated into English) (Independently Published/Amazon KDP-Available through Amazon).

Vasileiou, Ioannis (2019e), *European Union and Energy-The Route towards 2050-Thoughts, ideas and conclusions* (The Greek edition translated into English) (Independently Published/Amazon KDP-Available through Amazon).

Vasileiou, Ioannis (2019f), *European Union Trade: Trade Relations with Central Africa, the Southern African Development Community, Central America, the Andean Community and South Korea* (Independently Published/ Amazon KDP-Available through Amazon).

Vasileiou, Ioannis (2019g), *Health in the European Union: Member States-Agencies-Policies: Thoughts and Suggestions for the Present and the Future* (Independently Published/Amazon KDP-Available through Amazon).

Vasileiou, Ioannis (2019h), *Mercosur: Past, Present and Future of Integration in South America-Trade and Economic Relations with the European Union* (Independently Published/Amazon KDP-Available through Amazon).

Vasileiou, Ioannis (2019i), *PALOP-TL: The Portuguese-speaking African Countries and Timor-Leste:*

History-*Economy-Trade* (Independently Published/
Amazon KDP-Available through Amazon).

Vasileiou, Ioannis (2019j), *Taxation and Fraud
Prevention in the European Union: Lessons Learned
and Future Prospects* (Independently Published/
Amazon KDP-Available through Amazon).

Vasileiou, Ioannis (2019k), *The Foreign and Security
Policy of the European Union: A Critical Approach*
(2nd fully revised edition) (The first edition was
published in Greek in 2015) (Independently Published/
Amazon KDP-Available through Amazon).

Vasileiou, Ioannis (2019l), *Vietnam and New Zealand:
The Profiles: History-Trade-Economy* (Independently
Published/Amazon KDP-Available through Amazon).

Vasileiou, Ioannis (2020a), *Bavaria and North Rhine-
Westphalia: The Key Driving Forces of Development in
Germany: A Critical Analysi*s (Independently Published/
Amazon KDP-Available through Amazon).

Vasileiou, Ioannis (2020b), *CARICOM: The Caribbean Power:
Member States-Economy-Trade-Integration* (Independently
Published/Amazon KDP-Available through Amazon).

Vasileiou, Ioannis (2020c), *COMESA: Common
Market and Integration in Africa: Member States-
Economy-Trade* (Independently Published/
Amazon KDP-Available through Amazon).

BIBLIOGRAPHY

Vasileiou, Ioannis (2020d), *Contemporary Political, Economic and Social Issues in North Africa, Asia and Oceania: A Scrupulous Examination of Algeria, Egypt, Bangladesh, India, Iran, Kuwait, Lebanon, Pakistan, Sri Lanka and Australia* (Independently Published/ Amazon KDP-Available through Amazon).

Vasileiou, Ioannis (2020e), *Estonia and Latvia: The Complete Profiles: Economy-Trade-History* (Independently Published/Amazon KDP-Available through Amazon).

Vasileiou, Ioannis (2020f), *Five Different Faces of Latin America: Chile-Cuba-Peru-Puerto Rico-Venezuela: A Conscientious Scrutiny* (Independently Published/ Amazon KDP-Available through Amazon).

Vasileiou, Ioannis (2020g), *Former USSR and Former Yugoslavia: What About Now?* (Independently Published/ Amazon KDP-Available through Amazon).

Vasileiou, Ioannis (2020h), *From Fiji to Papua New Guinea and From Tuvalu to Vanuatu: Economic Growth and Development in the Pacific* (Independently Published/ Amazon KDP-Available through Amazon).

Vasileiou, Ioannis (2020i), *Sahel-Horn of Africa-Gulf of Guinea: Thoughts and Suggestions for Poverty Eradication, Increased Security and Economic Growth* (Independently Published/Amazon KDP-Available through Amazon).

Vasileiou, Ioannis (2020j), *Small Size, Enormous*

Interest: A Critical Analysis of Andorra, the Faroe Islands, Iceland, Liechtenstein, Luxembourg, Malta, Monaco and San Marino (Independently Published/ Amazon KDP-Available through Amazon).

Vasileiou, Ioannis (2020k), *South Africa-Namibia-Botswana: Thoughts And Conclusions for a More Encouraging Future* (Independently Published/ Amazon KDP-Available through Amazon).

Vasileiou, Ioannis (2021a), *Azerbaijan, Georgia, Kyrgyzstan, Tajikistan, Turkmenistan and Uzbekistan: What About Now?* (Independently Published/ Amazon KDP-Available through Amazon).

Vasileiou, Ioannis (2021b), *Bhutan, Japan, Laos, Mongolia, Nepal and the Philippines: Are They Still As They Used To Be?* (Independently Published/ Amazon KDP-Available through Amazon).

Vasileiou, Ioannis (2021c), *Novaya Zemlya, the New Siberian Islands, Sakhalin and the Kuril Islands: A Thorough Examination* (Independently Published/ Amazon KDP-Available through Amazon).

Vasileiou, Ioannis (2021d), *The Kamchatka Peninsula, Irkutsk Oblast and the Republic of Sakha: Yesterday, Today and Tomorrow* (Independently Published/ Amazon KDP-Available through Amazon).

BIBLIOGRAPHY

World History 1 (1990), Educational
Greek Encyclopedia (in Greek).

World History 2 (1990), Educational
Greek Encyclopedia (in Greek).

Zajicek, Edward K., Steen, Todd P. and Domański,
S. Ryszard (1997), "The Reform of Higher
Economic Education in Poland", *The Journal of
Economic Education*, 28 (4), pp. 377-382.

Ziomek, Agnieszka (2010), "Economics Performance
and Institutional Economics in Poland After
1989", *The American Journal of Economics
and Sociology*, 69 (5), pp. 1553-1565.

IOANNIS VASILEIOU

BIOGRAPHY

Ioannis Vasileiou was born in Athens in 1978. In 2001, he was awarded his Ptychio (equivalent to Bachelor's degree) in Political Science and Public Administration from the University of Athens (Greece). In 2003, he was awarded his first Master's degree (International Political Economy) from the University of Warwick (UK). In 2005, he was awarded his second Master's degree (International Economic Management) from the University of Birmingham (UK). In 2011, he was awarded his PhD from the University of Birmingham (UK) with specialization in the economic and political aspects of the European Union's Regional Policy. Since 2011, he has been conducting academic research on issues related to the European Union and international politics and economics.